Alfred's Premier Piano Course

Dennis Alexander • Gayle Kowalchyk • E. L. Lancaster • Victoria McArthur • Martha Mier

Alfred's *Premier Piano Course* Pop and Movie Hits Book 4 includes familiar pieces that reinforce concepts included in Lesson Book 4. The music continues the strong pedagogical focus of the course while providing the enjoyment of playing familiar popular music.

The pieces in this book correlate page-by-page with the materials in Lesson Book 4. They should be assigned according to the instructions in the upper right corner of each page of this book. They also may be assigned as review material at any time after the student has passed the designated Lesson Book page. Pop and Movie Hits 4 also can be used to supplement any beginning piano method.

Allowing students to study music they enjoy is highly motivating. Consequently, reading and rhythm skills often improve greatly when studying pop and movie music. The authors hope that the music in Pop and Movie Hits 4 brings hours of enjoyment.

Edited by Morton Manus

Produced by
Alfred Music Publishing Co., Inc.
P.O. Box 10003
Van Nuys, CA 91410-0003
alfred.com

Printed in USA.

ISBN-10: 0-7390-7406-7
ISBN-13: 978-0-7390-7406-0

CONTENTS

Blue Moon

Music by Richard Rodgers
Lyrics by Lorenz Hart

Inspector Gadget
(Theme)

Words and Music by
Haim Saban and Shuki Levy

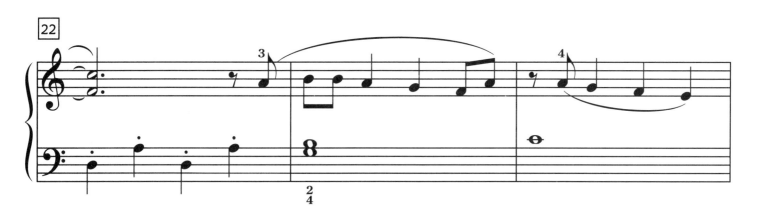

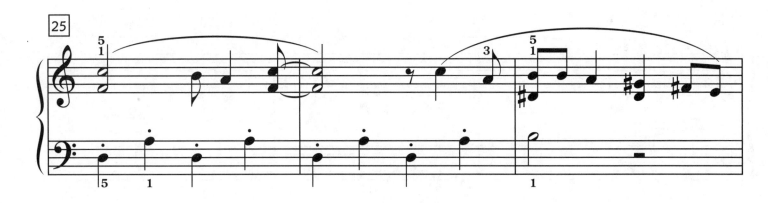

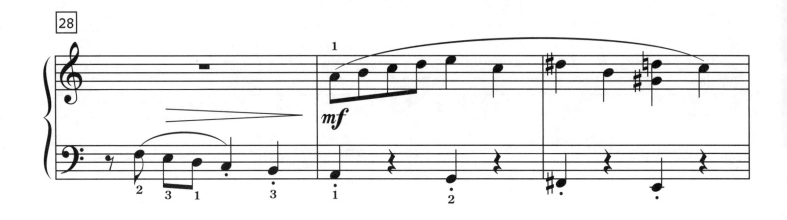

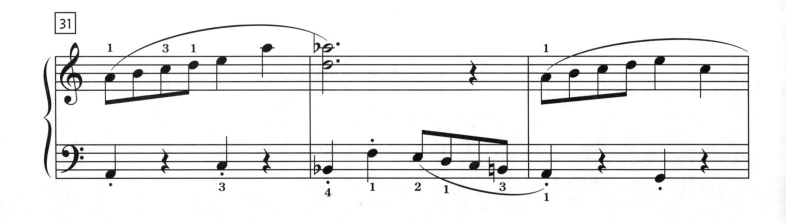

Gonna Fly Now
(Theme from *Rocky*)

By Bill Conti, Ayn Robbins and Carol Connors

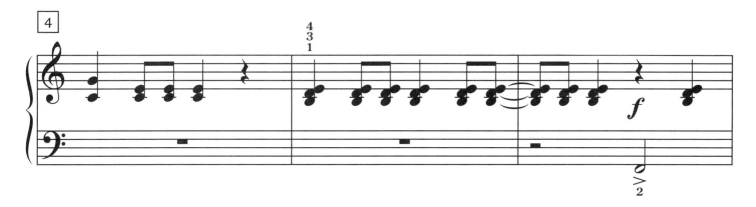

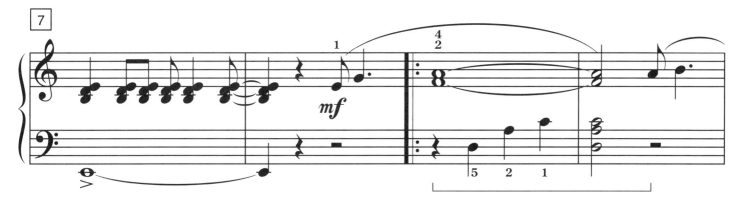

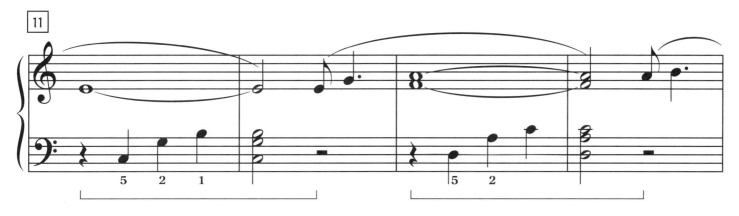

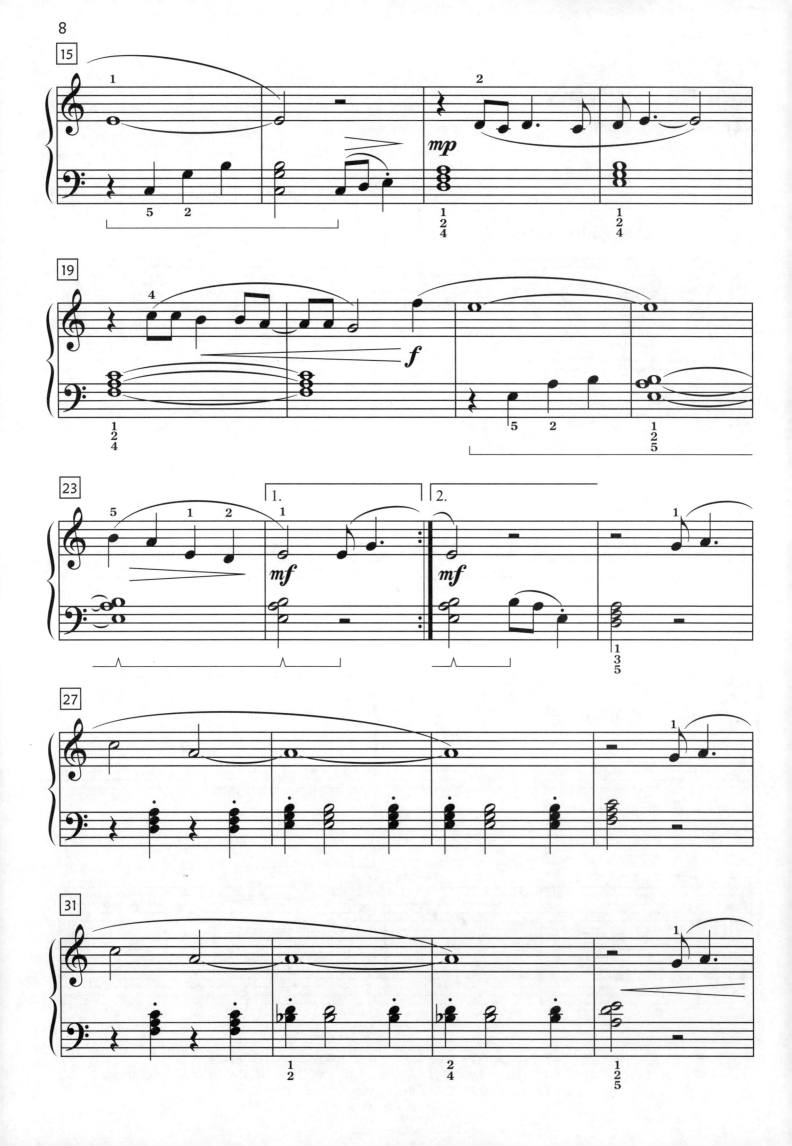

Endless Love

Words and Music by
Lionel Richie

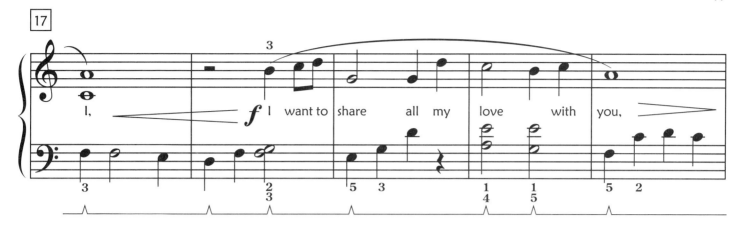

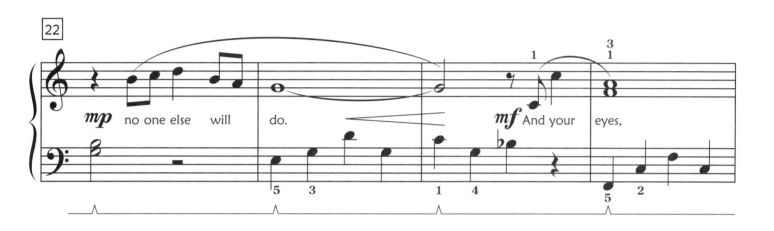

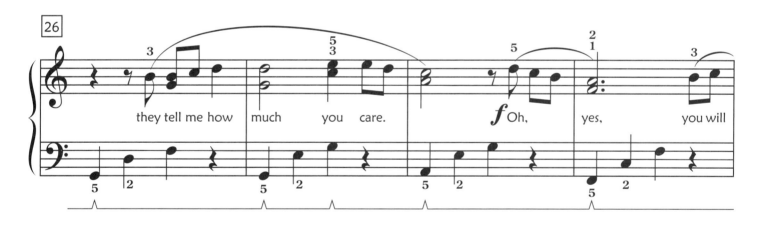

Lesson Book: pages 20–21

Theme from "Ice Castles"
(Through the Eyes of Love)

Music by Marvin Hamlisch
Lyrics by Carole Bayer Sager

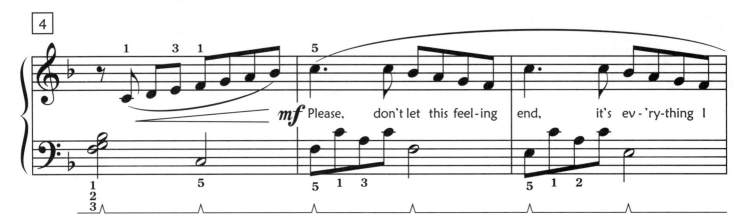

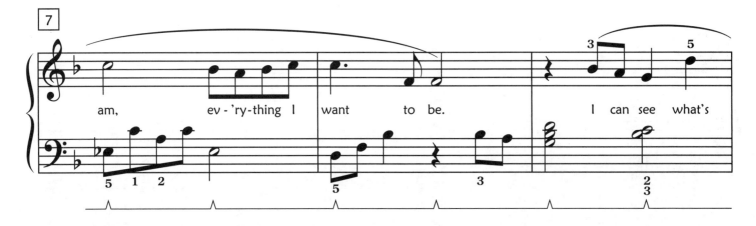

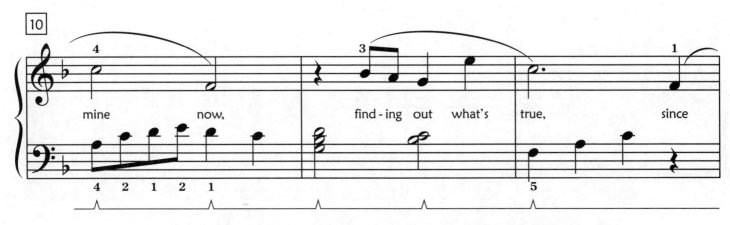

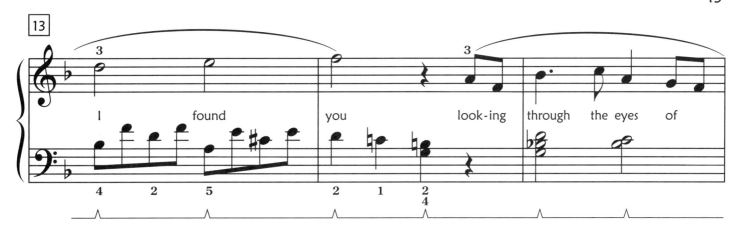

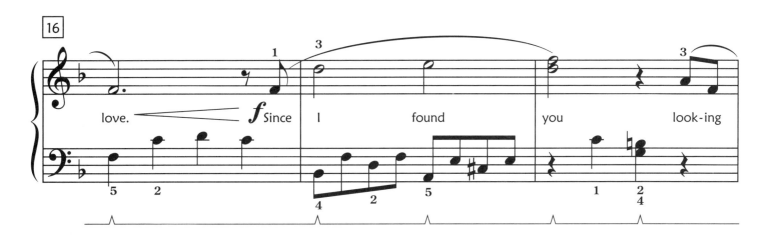

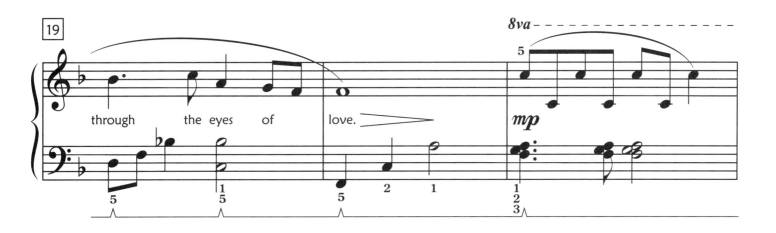

Batman Theme

Words and Music by
Neal Hefti

Steady rock tempo

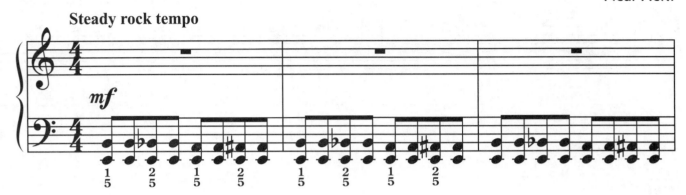

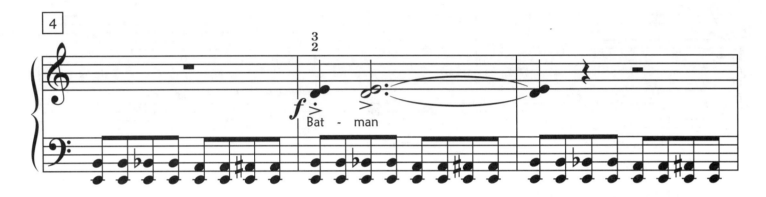

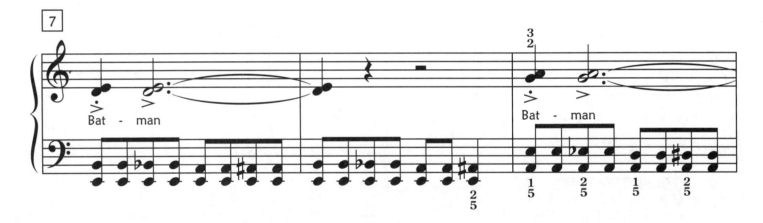

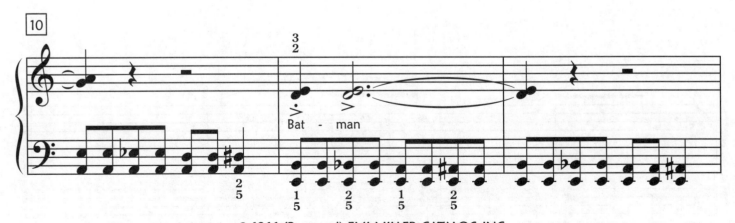

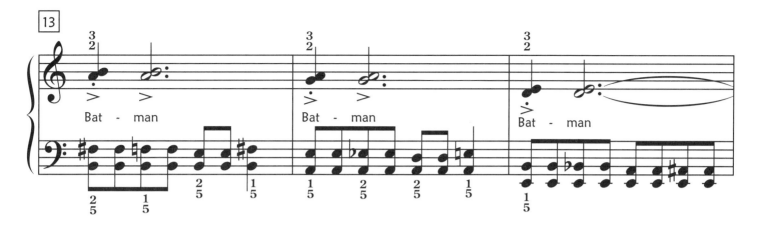

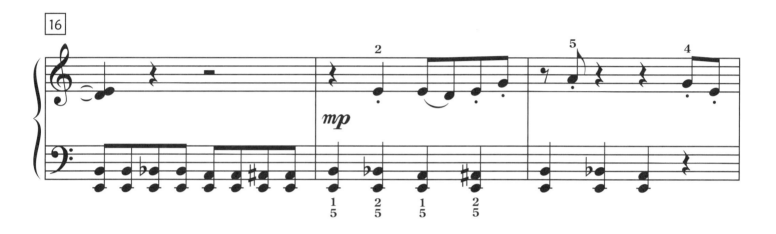

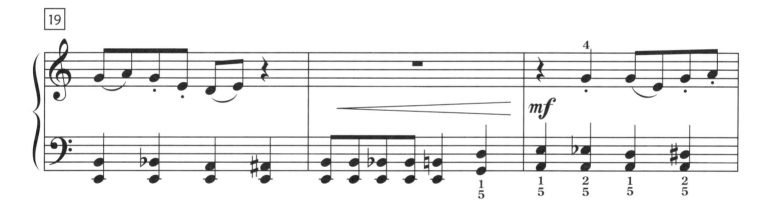

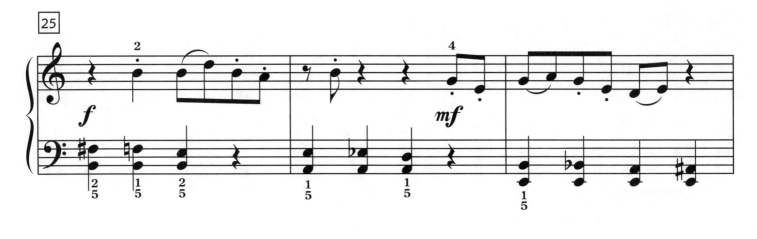

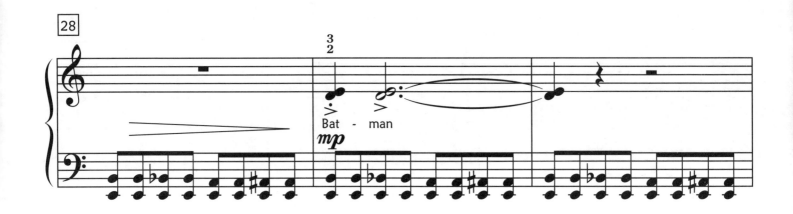

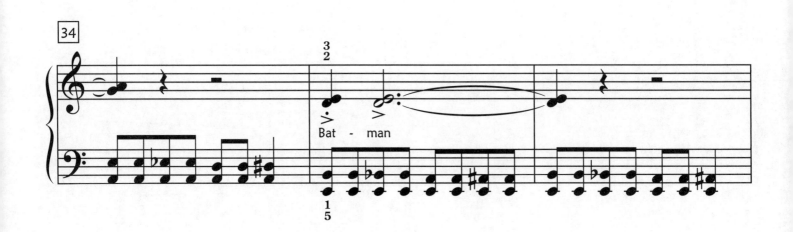

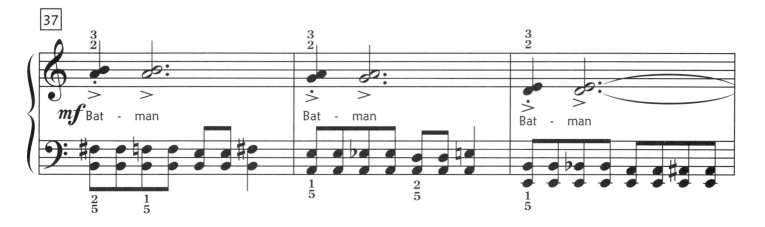

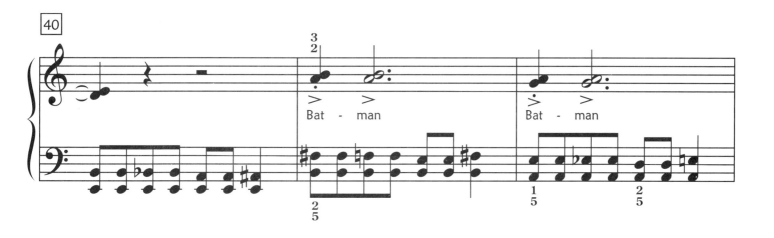

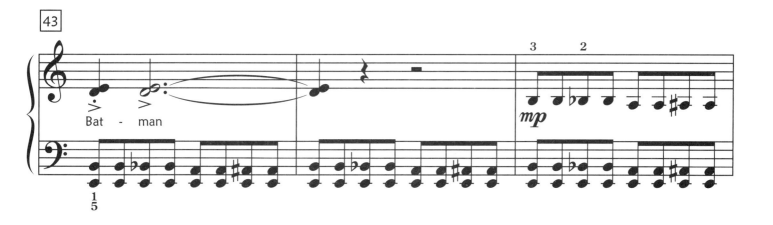

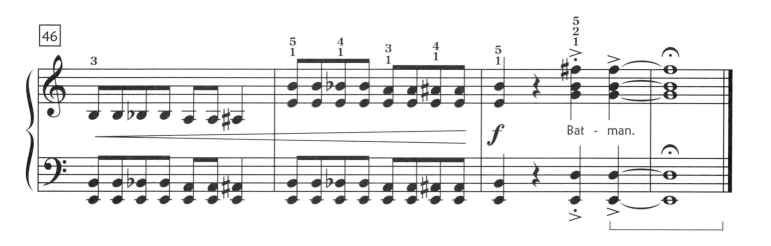

The Sound of Silence

Words and Music by
Paul Simon

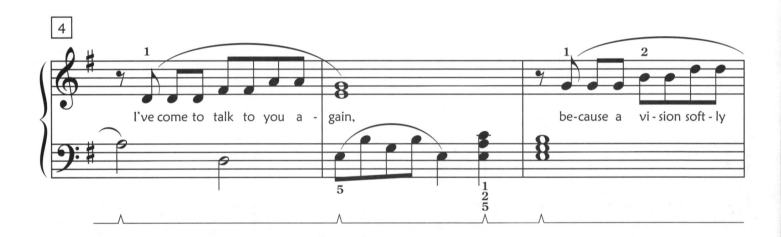

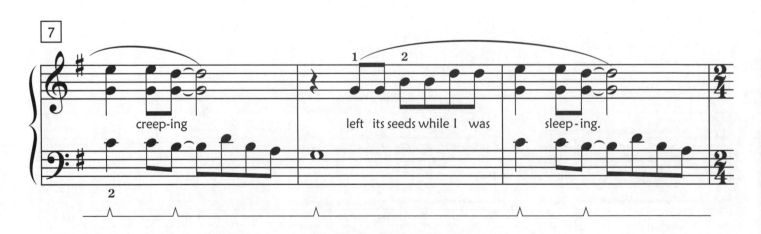

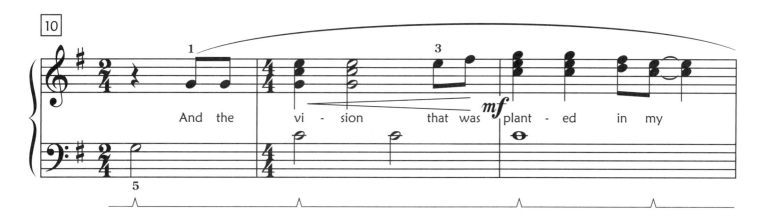

And the vi - sion that was plant - ed in my

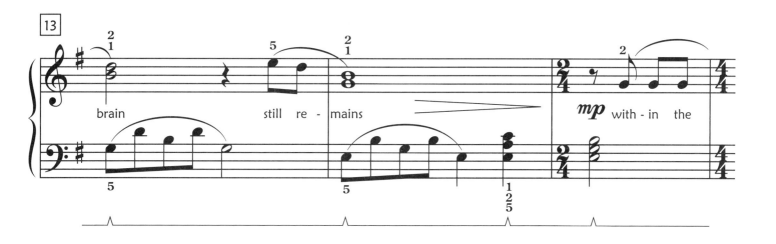

brain still re - mains with - in the

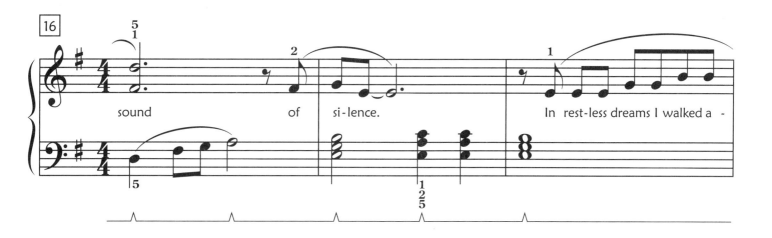

sound of si - lence. In rest-less dreams I walked a -

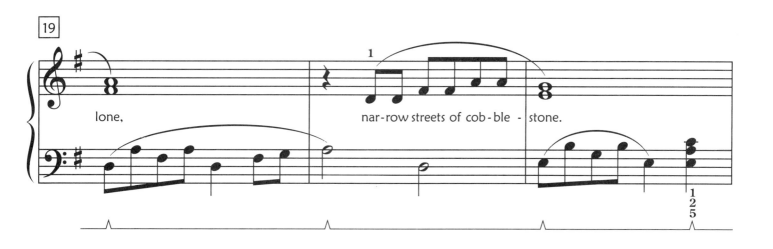

lone, nar-row streets of cob-ble - stone.

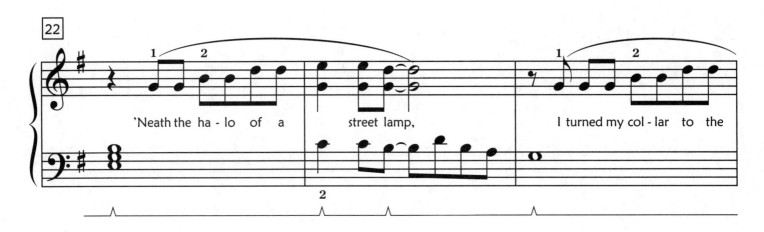

'Neath the ha - lo of a street lamp, I turned my col - lar to the

cold and damp when my eyes were stabbed by the

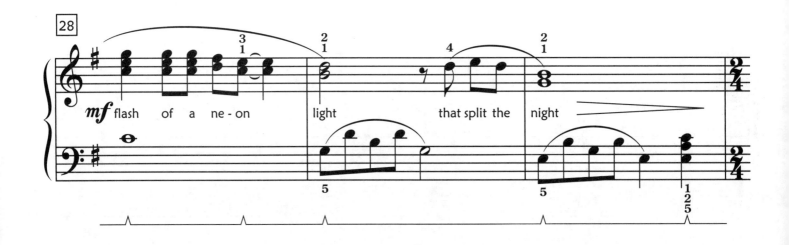

mf flash of a ne - on light that split the night

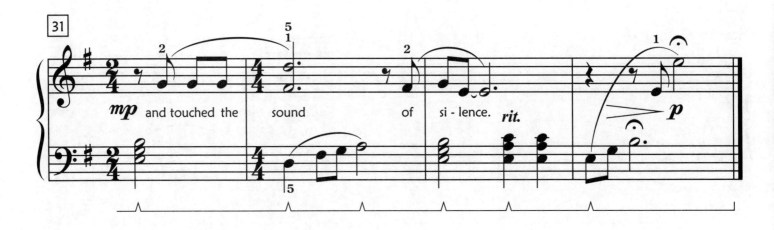

mp and touched the sound of si - lence. *rit.* *p*

Be Our Guest

(from Walt Disney's *Beauty and the Beast*)

Words by Howard Ashman
Music by Alan Menken

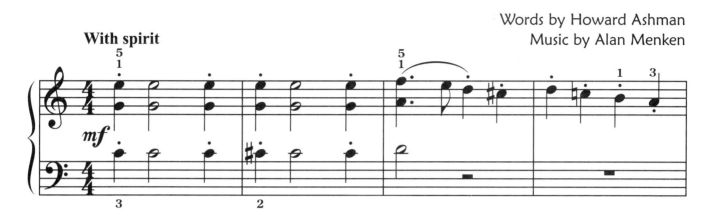

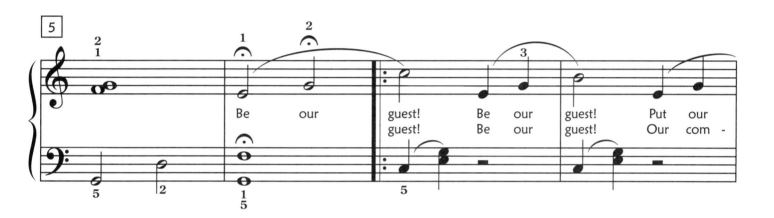

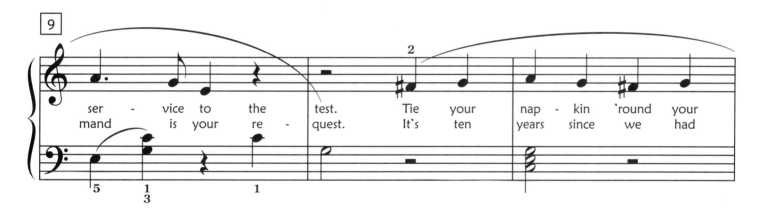

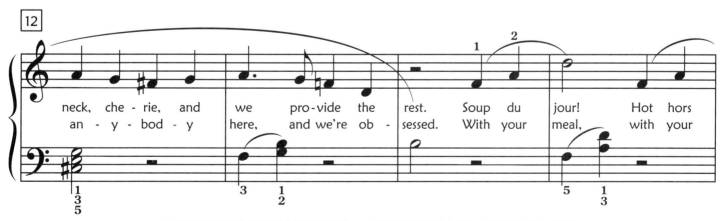

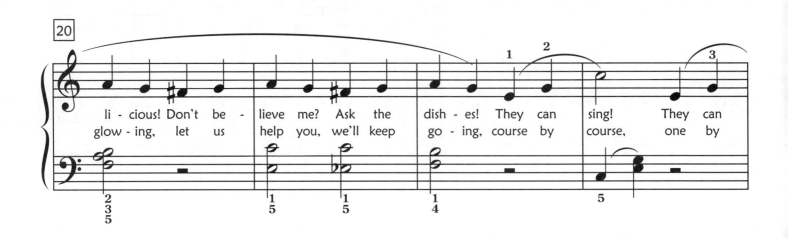

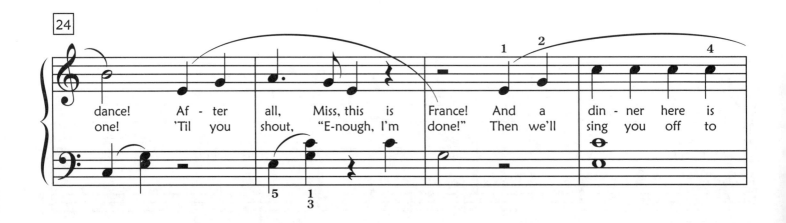

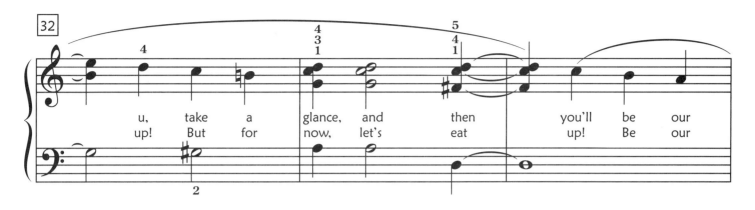

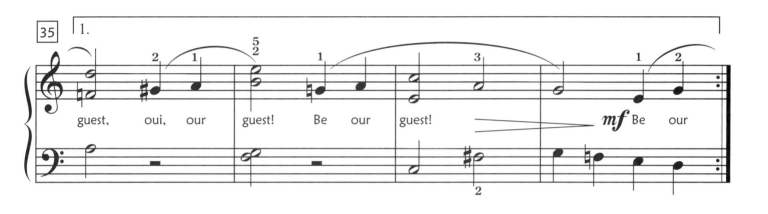

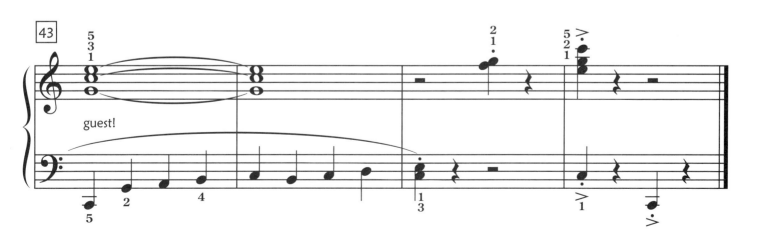

New Soul

Lesson Book: pages 36–37

Words and Music by
Yael Naim and David Donatien

Cruella De Vil
(from Walt Disney's *101 Dalmations*)

Words and Music by
Mel Leven

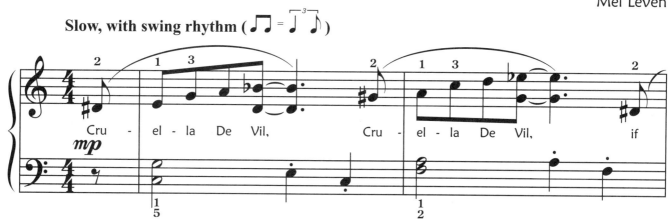

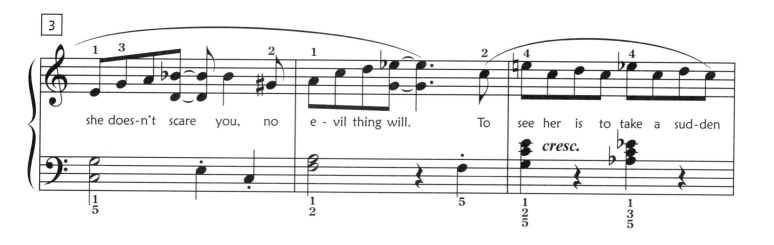

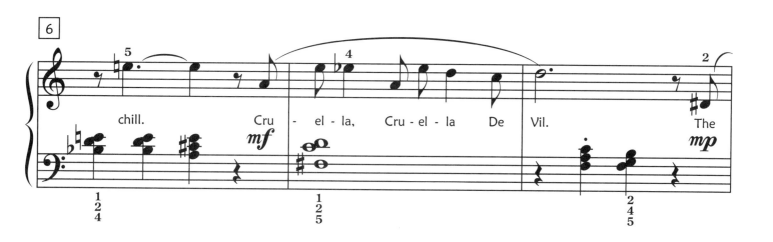

curl of her lips, the ice in her stare; all in - no - cent chil - dren had

bet - ter be - ware. She's like a spi - der wait-ing for the kill. Look

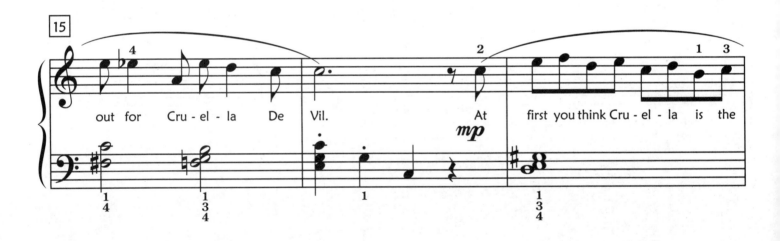

out for Cru - el - la De Vil. At first you think Cru - el - la is the

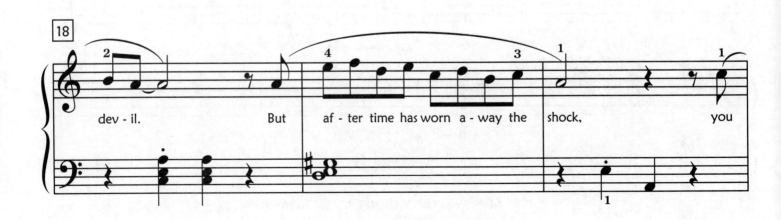

dev - il. But af - ter time has worn a - way the shock, you

come to re - al - ize you've seen her kind of eyes watch-ing you from un - der-neath a

rock. This vam - pire bat, this in - hu - man beast, she

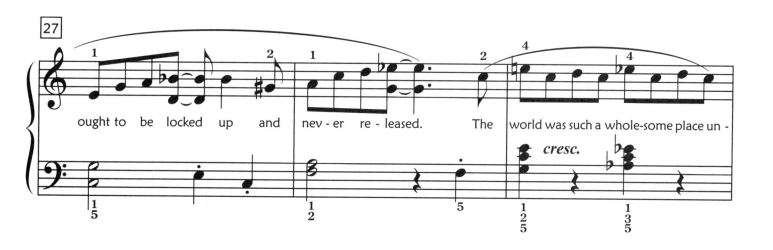

ought to be locked up and nev - er re - leased. The world was such a whole-some place un -

til Cru - el - la, Cru - el - la De Vil.

The Pink Panther

By Henry Mancini

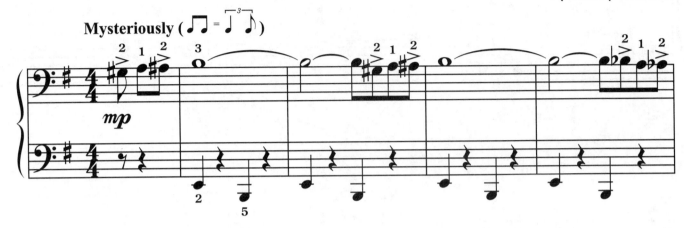

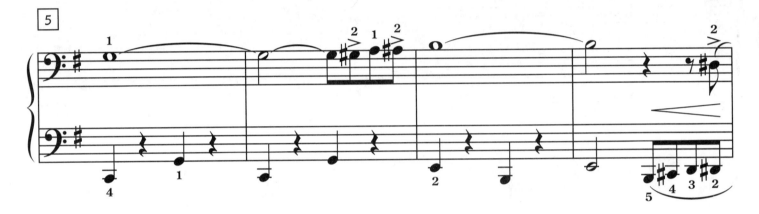

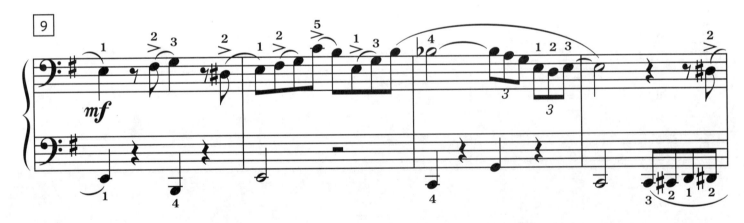